Job,

our contemporary. *sometime*

Job,
our contemporary

H. Harold Kent

William B. Eerdmans Publishing Company
Grand Rapids, Michigan

Copyright © 1967 by Wm. B. Eerdman's Publ. Co.
Library of Congress Catalog Card Number: 67-30116
ISBN: 0-8028-1106-X
Printed in the United States of America
Second printing, July 1973

Preface

The present day, chaotic with the after-math of universal cataclysm and fearful under the imminent threat of worse to come, has bred a race of thinkers whose salient characteristics are depression, despondency and despair. It is natural then, and logical, that the life and writings of the melancholy Sören Kierkegaard, of the demon-racked Feodor Dostoievsky, and of the tortured Nietzsche should fascinate serious-minded contemporaries of this mad world, and of their own torn and fragmented souls. Nor is it to be wondered at that such an existen-tialist philosophy as was undreamed of by Kierkegaard—openly atheistic and consist-ing in an "encounter with nothingness"—should attract many who swallow with avidity the outpourings of Jean-Paul Sartre,

Simone de Beauvoir and their school. Of
equal appeal, but to deeper natures, are the
philosophies of Heidegger, Jaspers and Mar-
cel, while many more are seeking to face
the conditions of human existence bravely
and realistically; if not "to see life steadily
and see it whole," at least to "beat their
music out" in a manner worthy of man
who is characterized—as Pascal, that Christian existentialist, put it—by "grandeur and
misery."

Finding myself in my dual capacity of
minister and architect, my double life of
preacher and man of affairs, increasingly
faced with questing souls and forced to
deal with my own doubts, I have been
driven back as always upon the Scriptures.
I have listened to the challenging cry of the
father of the faithful, Abraham: "Shall not
the Judge of all the earth do right?" I have
heard the psalmist complain that "the
wicked flourish like the green bay tree,"
and the prophet agonizingly expostulate,
"O Lord, how long shall I cry, and Thou
wilt not hear?" I have found myself
plunged into the "vanity of vanities, all is
vanity" of Koheleth, the Preacher in Eccle-

siastes. Above all I have found the experiences of the "patient," but very impatient
Job, and of Jeremiah the prophet of tears,
to be as up-to-date as tomorrow morning's
newspaper. Having discovered by careful
reading and rereading that all contemporary human questions were asked—and re-
ceived their answers, not necessarily in phil-
osophic terms, but in actual living—by
these ancient men of melancholy, I have
presented my personal understanding of
their respective messages, first from the
pulpit to my own congregations, and now
in this written form.

I am well aware that much present-day
superficial thinking and anti-Christian prop-
aganda parrots the egotistic skeptics of a
past generation such as the late George
Bernard Shaw, to whom "Job's God . . . is
a very bad debater" who "replies to the
patriarch's problem of the existence of evil
and its incompatibility with omnipotent
benevolence" by "jeering at him for being
unable to create a whale or to play with it
as a bird." Shaw further speaks of "pious
forgery" to conceal the fact that the origi-
nal poem left the problem of evil unsolved

and Job's criticism unanswered. I can only say that Shaw's "Black Girl in Search of God," in which those criticisms occur, seems to me as superficial as Voltaire's writing did to John Wesley. I turn back from it to Job to seek and to find some solid ground to rest my mind upon.

—H. Harold Kent

Contents

9

1

Adversity Versus Integrity

Many people, particularly believing Christians, have spoken to me during recent months out of the depth of their own experience, revealing the tragic sense of life that seems typical of the age in which we live. Of these, Job is surely the prototype.

Throughout the history of the Church of Christ, and among the Jewish people long before our era, there has been much debate as to the theme of the Book of Job. There is a general impression that it was written to answer the question: Why do the godly suffer? Long before my time or yours, however, people have exclaimed, "Well, if that is the purpose the book is a failure," for nowhere does it explain to anyone's satisfaction why the godly do suffer.

Certain aspects of the story seem to me

particularly relevant to the present day, to
our own circumstances. The now universal-
ly familiar word "existential" speaks of the
existence that is mine as an individual, the
impact of the facts of life upon my personality and my response to those facts. What
has the Word of God to say of the practical
situation that faces me individually? Exis-
tentially the Book of Job has much to say
to us of this age. The themes that suggest
themselves first, Adversity Versus Integrity
and The Sickness Unto Death, may bring us
mixed comfort, for no Christian lives deeply without discovering the paradox that
Job faced. We too exercise our faith, we
state in dogmatic terms what we believe;
then, to our dismay, we find that these
beliefs do not square with reality or cover
all the facts. Somehow the comforts of
belief by no means exclude periods of distress or even despair, because there are
poignant, unanswered problems insistently
demanding answer. So with Job in his pro-
longed agony. Yet, in this great account of
his experience there are also recorded fore-
gleams of the all-sufficiency of the Divine
grace, and outbursts of the poetry of pure

faith in God. The book indeed reveals to us
the essential nature of true faith. That is its
supreme revelation—the deep nature of
real, abiding, God-engendered faith.

An old poem asks of the famous Battle
of Blenheim, "and what good came of it at
last?" That is the question asked, and that
is the question answered, in the Book of
Job; but the purpose of the drama is found
in its total context. It culminates in the
great revelation that God gives to the patriarch and in the patriarch's response to the
theophany. Not until the very end of the
book is its real message and ministry made
known. All the events, the commonplace,
everyday happenings, the disasters described in the first two chapters, the unveiling of scenes revelatory of heavenly activi-
ties behind this human scene, the expres-
sions of Job's friends, Job's rebuttal of
their arguments: all these must be viewed
in the light of the final revelation, of God's
unveiling of Himself and man's ultimate
response to his God.

There is not a book in the world so
fraught with dramatic psychological insight. By the Holy Spirit's inspiration the

writer withholds his climax to the end;
then, and not until then, is the secret of his
intention made known. In a very real sense
what, for want of a better term, we
might call the Godhead of God, or His
essential Deity, is there set forth in an
overwhelming grandeur that brings the human being into silent awe and reverence
before Him.

The book is also a revelation of essential
manhood, and of the precise nature of the
relationship of a God who is truly God
with a man who is truly man. This is shown
to be a relationship of grace, which is ap-
prehended by faith, a faith that works in
obedience and trust.

Again from this book we discover that
the Holy Spirit, who inspired the writer, is
concerned with man *as* man, separated
from his environment. Job is snatched
away from his family circle. Literally, his
family circle is snatched away from him.
His whole society is shattered and he stands
alone. Separated from history, he stands
forsaken in an alien cosmos. There he
stands as a concrete personal example, the
very stuff of human life, delineated sharply

and compellingly in an existential situation. He is representative of the entire human species. He is not a Jew. He may have been an Edomite, for Uz is thought to have been situated in Edom, but all national and racial distinction is wiped out in this story. There are no distinctions, no cultural divisions, no political or even religious parties. Here is a man completely alone. All the peculiarities of humankind are transcended, and as he transcends these differences, so over the centuries and millennia has Job transcended time itself.

Look at him, then. For the purpose for which the Holy Spirit singles him out, he is a model of the most uncommon integrity, pressed by the most extreme adversity.

His integrity? "There was a man in the land of Uz whose name was Job; and that man was blameless and upright, one who feared God, and eschewed evil." To this statement his wife added her testimony when she said: "Do you still retain your integrity?" He was integral within himself— he was a whole man. Within his environment his relationships were of the right kind, toward himself and toward his fam-

ily, because they were primarily directed
toward his God.

One of his customs, sketched in a few
enlightening words, reveals something of
his character, for we are told that on family
festal occasions Job offered sacrifice on
behalf of his children, one offering for each
child in the family, lest "my sons have
sinned" against the Lord.

Sometimes Job is criticized for self-
righteousness. But when, by the testimony
of God, this man was blameless and upright, a God-fearer who turned away from
evil, then legitimately and naturally a sense
of rightness possessed him. The New Testament would speak of it as "a conscience
void of offence." Job was unconscious of
being offensive to God or to his fellow
men. Therefore the state of the man at the
beginning is one of tranquility and health,
not only physical health, but wholeness of
body and spirit. Finally, to complete the
picture in Old Testament terms, the blessing of God was on the man in wealth, in his
happy and full home, in a piety matching
his morality. He was a whole man.

Now adversity meets that integrity. Job

experienced blow after blow, falling upon him until he was stripped of everything that man holds dear in life, his "worldly possessions" as we call them. Next his family was snatched away, and then loathsome disease took possession of him. Surely he could not have been reduced to a lower state! His wife said, "I should get rid of my integrity if I were you! This God you talk about! I'd renounce a God like that! I should have nothing to do with such a God. Why don't you commit suicide and get out of it all?" Do you realize that that is the import of what she said? "Do you still retain your integrity? Curse God and die—and get out of all your troubles. That is the only advice I can give you." So the man stands absolutely alone. His three friends? No one who reads this book, no one especially who has shared in some measure Job's experience, will fail to realize that the presence of such friends intensified his loneliness.

And at this point the writer, by the Spirit of God, lifts Job to the realm of psychological reality and portrays the disintegration of his integrity, the anatomy of

his despair. Job and his three friends sat
facing each other day after day, until finally he could stand the reproof of their silence no longer, and he broke out with his
terrible complaint.

First, he uttered a curse on the day of
his conception and on the day of his birth.
"Let the day perish wherein I was born."
Dr. Alexander Whyte used to say that all
great souls are melancholy souls. The longer I live the more I realize that his dictum
was correct. There are far more of God's
own people in these days who have descended the depths than perhaps at any
other time in the history of the Church of
Christ, or of the world in which the Church
finds her place. Why? It is in search of an
answer to that question that I have turned
to the Book of Job. Why are there so many
who say: "Yes, I know that the Lord Jesus
is my Saviour. I know that I have eternal
life in Him. I believe that it shall be well
with my soul—but somehow, here and now,
the problems I face that are insoluble, the
burdens I bear that are intolerable, the enemies I meet who are undefeatable, my own
utter weakness and perplexity, the posses-

sion of my soul by God-given desires which can never be satisfied: all these things, the frustration and the agony of life, overwhelm me. I do not doubt the eternal verities. There is a sense in which I know something of the joy of the Lord as my strength: yet somehow everything is wrong. Why did God ever bring me to birth? Why *am* I?" Even so Job began his complaint.

Beginning with this Why, he moved on to the query: Why Not? "Why did I not die at birth? Then I should have lain down and been quiet, I should have slept, I could have been at rest. There the wicked cease from troubling; there the weary are at rest." People have told me that they never have had a desire for death. If not, unless they are very young, they have not lived very deeply. My first reaction to the terrible news of President Kennedy's assassination was a yearning to die, because I belonged to a race characterized by this kind of evil. Nausea possessed me. A colleague of mine, a man who did very noble work in the Polish underground against both the Germans and the Russians, told me that he could not eat any dinner that evening because of physical revulsion at the news. I was surprised, for during his commando days he had killed a good many men and had seen death in terrible forms. "That was war," he said; "but this was different!" It is this nausea at evil which takes possession of those who face seriously the human race in its present distress. This attitude ought to be the characteristic of the more thoughtful of God's people, and it does indeed characterize very many. Therefore they cry, as Job cried, Why did I not die at birth?

Then he goes on to another Why? "Why is light given to him that is in misery?" Here, and increasingly all the way through, Job is wrestling with the ultimate mystery of Divine governance. God is governing his life, but *how* is He governing it? Where can he see the Divine hand in it? Why does God do things in this way? That is the great problem. Yet, even so, a mystery of Divine grace permeates the entire book, never allowing him to be finally alienated from God, the Divine Protagonist. And there are flashing insights of revelation penetrating, by the Holy Spirit, through the depths of his pathos, through the depths of his despair, through the depths of his melancholy, into his heart and life.

There are mysteries so poignant, so agonizingly evil in their impact upon us, that if not solved they would seem to demonstrate, not the righteousness, but the unrighteousness of God. And the solutions are NOT given in this life. Job stood alone. His three companions had been his friends for a long time. All through the years they had had no cause to criticize him adversely. He stood behind them and before them in his integrity, a man of God, a man with love for his fellows, a man who in every respect was admirable. Yet now all they could do was sit in judgment upon him. Not one of them took his part. But suddenly he was lifted up by the Holy Spirit, and cried, "Behold!", literally, "See, look!" We get the sense of it, the shock, the arrest of attention if we translate it so. Job suddenly cried, "See, look, my Witness is in heaven." God spoke through him, God the Holy Spirit. Out of the abysmal depth and the gloom he cried: "I have a Vindicator, I have One who stands for me in the heaven-

ly places." So strikingly was the revelation
given that he dared to call on God Himself
and say, "Lay down a pledge for me with
Thyself."

That is a tremendous word: "Lay down
a pledge for me with Thyself." For though
he did not know it, that is exactly what
God has done. God has become surety,
pledge for my vindication, for the sequel in
eternity, for the fulfilment of my every
God-engendered desire and my every need.
The security is the pledge He has Himself
given in the Person of His own Son, whom
He yielded up for us; and now the Pledge is
at the right hand of God, the Man in glory.
Job could not know it—we can.

I am staggered by the faith of these Old
Testament saints! Think of Abraham, who,
we are told, had this kind of God, "a God
who gives life to the dead and calls the
things that are not as though they were."
When he went to sacrifice Isaac, he believed
that God would raise him up, even from
the dead. Then we talk about our faith!
Nobody had ever been raised from the dead
in Abraham's day. Not a word of Scripture
had yet been written. There was not one of

the historical facts recorded with which
you and I bolster our faith. Yet Abraham
stood before God, called Him "the Judge
of all the earth who must do right," and
believed in a God who can raise the dead.

The man Job sat there, stripped of everything, utterly hopeless and helpless. Re-
cently I had about three weeks in which,
due to dermatitis, I had not a single night's
sleep. Night after night I sat on the edge of
the bed, covered with itching sores from
head to foot, knowing something of how
Job must have felt. Thank God I had no
friends like his there to bother me—at least
I was all alone! I couldn't have taken what
Job had to. But there, the most pitiable
object imaginable, he dared say to God:
"Lay down a pledge for me with Thyself."
And his pleading went on and outward and
became more intense until at last he cried,
"I KNOW that my Redeemer liveth and
that He shall stand in the latter day upon
the earth." Ah, what an insight of revelation—what a flash of Divine grace! This
man was able, in that awful situation, to
say, "I have a Redeemer, I have a living
Redeemer. I have a Redeemer who one day

is going to stand upon earth on my behalf."

Surely, no matter in what depths you and I find ourselves, there is a message here for us. We have a ten-thousand-fold greater knowledge of God and of His grace than Job ever had. We have the full-orbed revelation of God's love in Jesus Christ, in His Person and in His work for our salvation. Yet how often we feel sorry for ourselves. What victims we are of our own self-pity— how seldom we rise to the place of saying: I know.

Do you find yourself distressed in these strange days in which we live? Is life perplexed and frustrating? Does pressure from the enemy without, and especially from the enemy within, bear heavily? Are you filled from time to time with the tragic sense of life? Though you are God's child you cannot surmount it; and it sometimes overwhelms you. It is all very well, you feel, to talk about the "joy of the Lord" being your "strength" or to repeat the Apostle's great word, "Rejoice in the Lord always; and again I say unto you, Rejoice"; but you seem unable to do it more than occasionally. These agonies, the pathos of life,

the distress, the enemies that you face, the
evil from within, all these, in our rushing,
heartless days, press and depress you. Is
that so? Then I introduce you to a man
who in ancient days was dealt with by God
that he might become an example to you
and me. We have not looked behind the
scenes at the power of evil, at Satan and his
design. We have not looked at the throne of
heaven, the court of the Most High God,
and the determinations that were made
there. I have simply sought to bring you
this man in his integrity, then in his adversity, and to show the first impact of that
adversity upon his integrity.

2

Sickness Unto Death

The Tragic Sense of Life is the title of a
book by a Spanish novelist philosopher,
Miguel de Unamuno. It seems to me to
describe perfectly the experiences of Job.
Similarly the title, "The Sickness Unto
Death," from another great thinker, Sören
Kierkegaard, suggests itself as describing
the next stage in Job's experience. The
sickness unto death, Kierkegaard said, is
despair. That is the sickness from which
Job came to suffer.

The most evident, the most apparent and
obvious phases of Job's difficulties, his suffering and adversity, did not bring about
the sickness unto death. This fact is clear
from the narrative. Suddenly and unex-
pectedly everything was shattered, destitution was complete. The man erstwhile of

wealth and authority had been stripped of everything and was levelled with the veriest pauper; but his immediate reaction to those disasters did not constitute the sickness unto death, nor render him a victim of despair.

On a deeper plane, his sorrow consisted in sore bereavement: seven sons and three daughters had been destroyed by a lightning stroke of natural force; yet that complete bereavement did not in itself cause the sickness unto death. Neither did his divorce from his wife, because such it was on the real plane, the plane of sympathetic understanding. In the hour when he most needed her (she, poor woman, had suffered as he had) she said, "Why have a God like that, why stay with your integrity? Renounce it and renounce God." So, on the deepest plane, the plane of moral and spiritual oneness, Job suffered divorce from the one who was nearest to him. But that, in itself and in its effect, did not constitute the sickness unto death.

If neither utter destitution nor bereavement and divorce, then most certainly his physical problems, the agony he was suffer-

ing in the body, even at its worst, did not
constitute the sickness unto death. How
then did it come about?

At the end of the first phase, when all
this had befallen him, we find him in complete perplexity, frustration, and agony of
mind, questioning without finding answer.
Yet despair did not take possession of him
at any of these stages. Nor was it caused by
his three "friends"—a word I put in quota-
tion marks, for when Job said "Miserable
comforters are you all," he has my sympa-
thy. "Why don't you stay home and leave
me alone?" he implied. Their complete misunderstanding of him and all that he represented, as well as all that he had suffered,
their consequent condemnation, implying
that secretly he had been a great sinner—
that fact alone could explain the experience he had undergone!—and therefore his
absolute isolation from his fellows: these
consequences of his sufferings were not the
sickness unto death.

The sickness unto death went far deeper
than that. It consisted in a sense of
estrangement from God Himself. Job,
knowing already enough of God to be able

to evaluate his loss, had come (at just what
stage we are not told) in the agony of those
experiences, in the travail of those horrible
days, to the place where he had lost touch
with God. He was isolated from Him, although reminded by memory of the comfort that faith in Him once brought.

If Job could only have said, as did the
German philosopher Nietzsche (who,
though insane, appraised his times better
than did all the contemporary optimists),
"God is dead!" it might have been easier
for him. But he clung to his belief in the
Deity. Somehow he knew that God is, that
God is just and that God is omnipotent.
That was the curse of it. That was what
rendered him utterly despairing. "If God is
just, why does this happen to me? If He is
all-powerful, why does He not do something about my case?" Do you wonder why
I turn to the story of Job? It is because I
have of late been shocked into a realization
that this book is up-to-the-minute, that
these are the experiences of a vast number
in our own day.

The alternative possible to a great many
lighter souls was not possible to Job: the

alternative of unbelief, of skepticism, of
agnosticism, of saying that he did not and
could not know. This inability to find the
relief of atheism is the sickness unto death.
If in your agony of heart, when the founda-
tions are destroyed and everything goes by
the board, you could only say: "God is
dead; there is no God. I cannot and do not
believe," it might be much easier for you,
but you cannot say that nor could Job. If
he could have, then the essential problem
would have ceased to trouble him. He still
would have been suffering physically—still
grappling morally with undeserved evil.
That would have remained, but the spiritual torture would have ended. There
would have been no sickness unto death,
no ultimate despair gripping his soul.

Note the path of Job's agony. Often
lately I have repeated to myself Rudyard
Kipling's couplet which Alexander Whyte
was very fond of quoting.

> "Down to Gehenna and up to the Throne,
> He travels the fastest who travels alone."

But Job's path was not a straight path

down to Gehenna—certainly it was not a
straight one up to the Throne. He was not
plunged into the abyss to remain there. It
was an up-and-down affair, a movement
incessantly alternating: first he was on the
mountain top, almost immediately to be
plunged into the depths of the valley. His
psychological casebook would be a zigzag
or a seesaw. The sickness unto death, indeed!

Nowhere in all sacred literature, scarcely
anywhere in all secular literature, is there
such doubt as Job expresses; but Tennyson
would have agreed with him:

> "There lies more faith in honest doubt,
> Believe me, than in half the creeds."

Job was obsessed with such doubt as has
seldom been described by voice or pen; yet
almost immediately doubt ended and certi-
tude took its place, once again to disappear
when doubt came to the fore.

Not in all Scriptural literature is there
another such human rebel revolting against
God and His government. A later Scripture
says: "You have heard of the patience of

Job." So we have a mistranslation which
has become a cliché. The word actually
means endurance; in effect, "You have
heard how Job had to take it"! This trans-
lation solves a long-standing puzzle, because it is the impatience of Job that char-
acterizes most of his statements. The ninth
chapter is typical of his attitude: revolt, yet
at the very moment of declaring that he is a
rebel, accepting whatever God will bring
into his life. Once again the attitude of
acceptance departs and once again he is in
revolution against the government of God.
He is seen wrestling as a man wrestles in the
ring with his adversary, struggling against
his God, yet declaring that all his hope is in
Him. He is in flight from God, yet longing
to encounter Him as an I to a Thou. Such
spiritual ambivalence is the curse and the
experience of a great many of us in this
day.

In this man and in the book that pre-
sents him there is a deep belief and hope
and longing, but it is all misguided. He had,
alternating with their opposites, all three.
He was a man of faith despite his unbelief.
He was a man of hope, despite the grip of

despair. He was a man of longing, although all ambition and all prospects had departed. But the secret of this man's problem is that while he believed and hoped and longed, it was not in God but in his own concept of God.

That perhaps is our trouble. We say: I have trusted in God; my hope has been in Him. God knows that I've longed for Him. I have experienced what Augustine said: Thou hast made us for thyself and our hearts can never find rest until they rest in Thee; but He has failed me and I find no satisfaction. Yet in reality it is not God but our conception of God in which we have been hoping and trusting with longing. This fact is evident in Job's case.

At the end of the story Job said, "I had heard of Thee by the hearing of the ear, but now my eye seeth Thee; wherefore I abhor myself and repent in dust and ashes." Before that, his *notion* of God was the subject of his faith and his hope and his desire. He is a man of aspiration; he aspires to meet God, but on his own terms. All the way through, his aim is that his integrity shall be vindicated. He stands up to God and asks: "Why does this happen to me? Why do you let this occur in my life? I am a righteous man." He wants to meet God in order that God may pat him on the back and say, "There, there, Job, you are everything you say you are. I am sorry that this sort of thing has happened to you." That is precisely the attitude of Job and of most of us in our dealings with God.

His theology was correct as far as it went. There is many a revelation in Job's words of the creative power and wisdom of the Almighty, of God in providence, in the innermost governance of individual life, of God as Sovereign, as the ruler of all. Job's theology was completely orthodox. Yet he used his sense of personal worth as a claim upon God: "My righteousness, my integrity, the man that I am." He was unable to reconcile his integrity with his fate. The whole story is integrity versus adversity, and Job could not reconcile the one with the other, any more than you and I can in our experience. Because he could not, he challenged God's justice, and indeed made himself the judge of his Creator. We must not forget the place Job assumed, for that is the essential sin: that I put myself in the place of judge and tell God how He ought to run my life.

Job fell into the sickness-unto-death, because to him his sufferings seemed to be out of all proportion to the pettiness of his failure. Here we must let the record speak for itself, and what it says is startling.

With recklessness born of despair, Job faces it out before God in language which the most determined apologist finds difficult to explain away and which most pious commentators prefer to ignore or tone down. "Thou (Job is speaking to God) writest bitter things against me; Thou makest me inherit the iniquities of my youth." I sowed my wild oats and now You are taking it out on me! "Thou puttest my feet in stocks and watchest all my path. Thou settest a bound for the soles of my feet. Man wastes away like a rotten thing, like a garment that is moth-eaten. Man that is born of woman is of few days, and full of trouble. He comes forth like a flower, and withers: he flees like a shadow, and continues not. And dost Thou open Thy eyes upon such a one and bring him into judgment with Thee?" In other words, man is just like a moth, a poor, trivial, foolish thing. Maybe he did sow his wild oats in youth. So what? Is he important enough for You to take notice of him and punish him?

"Who can bring a clean thing out of an unclean? There is not one. Since his days are determined, and the number of his months is with Thee, and Thou hast appointed his bounds that he cannot pass, look away from him, and desist, that he may enjoy, like a hireling, his day." That needs no comment from me! Job is speaking very plainly. Once again he says: "He crusheth me with a tempest and multiplieth my wounds without cause." I don't deserve it; there is no reason for this kind of thing! Once more, "Thou dost seek out my iniquities and search for my sin, although Thou knowest I am not guilty." When we are exalting Job, let us not overlook the fact that this is the way he talked to God. "You are unjust," he said, "You are unfair, You are wrong, You are a coward. I am not guilty and yet You punish me." Is not that attitude, less frankly admitted, character-

istic even of many Christians of our own
day?

Hear Job again. "And there is none to
deliver me out of Thy hands." And again.
"I hold fast my righteousness and I will not
let it go. My heart does not reproach me
for any of my days." Sanctimonious, self-
righteous humbug, isn't he, even as you and
I so often are. Then again, "Oh, that I had
the indictment (or my accusation) written
by my Adversary." God is his Adversary.
"Surely I would bind it to me like a crown,
I would give an account of all my steps;
like a prince I would approach Him." Have
you ever known anybody so full of what
my father used to call "stinking pride," as
this man Job? It permeates all his statements at this stage.

I was brought up to think that the great
characters of the Old Testament were mod-
els of perfection. Later, many years later, I
was given the key to the truth in the Epis-
tle of James, "These were men of like pas-
sions with ourselves," of like natures with
ourselves. How Job and you and I are akin
in many of these thoughts and attitudes!
So he makes God directly responsible for

his plight. "He will not let me get my breath, for He fills me with bitterness." "If it is a contest of strength, behold Him; if it is a matter of justice, who can summon Him"—that is, to the bar of justice,—"for trial?" Once again, "If I speak, my pain is not assuaged, and if I forbear, how much of it leaves me? Surely now God has worn me out; He has made desolate my company. And He has shrivelled me up, which is a witness against me; and my leanness has risen up against me, it testifies to my face. He has torn me in His wrath, and hated me; He has gnashed His teeth at me; my Adversary sharpens His eyes against me." "I was at ease, and he broke me asunder; He seized me by the neck and dashed me to pieces; He set me up as His target, and His archers surround me; He slashes open my kidneys, and does not spare; He pours out my gall on the ground, He breaks me with breach upon breach; He runs upon me like a warrior." Further down in the old version is a wonderful text often used: "Though He slay me, yet will I trust Him." The Revised Standard Version is nearer the Hebrew: "Behold (See, Look) He will slay me,"—I have no hope—"yet I will defend my ways to His face." Though He slay me and I am hopeless, I will declare my righteousness in the face of God.

Job surely is the Saul of Tarsus of the Old Testament, so completely sure of his own righteousness that even God cannot stand before him.

Once again let the record speak: "He has walled up my way so that I cannot pass; He has set darkness upon my path; He has stripped from me my glory and taken the crown from my head; He breaks me down on every side and I am gone, and my hope has He pulled up like a tree; He has kindled His wrath against me and counts me as His adversary." Again, "Behold He will slay me. If I sin, what do I do to Thee, Thou Watcher of men? Why hast Thou made me Thy mark? Why have I become a burden to Thee?"

These pleas, these cries, are to be found all the way through the book. The physical pain, the deprivation and bereavement and divorce, the misunderstanding and condemnation and ostracism, withal the theological, the spiritual anxiety concerning the

God who had been mocked—this created a persecution complex in Job and with it, inevitably, a personal-grandeur complex. Notice some of his declarations: "Thou dost renew Thy witnesses against me and increase Thy vexation toward me; Thou dost bring fresh hosts against me." In other words, "I'm standing alone in the universe. God hates me and He is bringing all this evil upon me." It was Nietzsche before his time, a forerunner of William Cowper's obsession that out of all the God-lovers, he alone was damned eternally by the mere fiat of that electing God.

Once again, "He breaks me with breach upon breach, He runs upon me like a warrior, although there is no violence in my hands and my prayer is pure. Troops come together, they cast up siegeworks against me, and they camp around about my tent. He has put my brethren far from me and acquaintances are wholly estranged from me. My kinsfolk and my close friends have failed me; the guests in my house have forgotten me; my maidservants count me as a stranger; I have become an alien in their eyes. I call to my servant but he gives me no answer; I am repulsive to my wife, loathsome to the sons of my own mother. Even young children despise me; when I rise they talk against me. Have pity on me, have pity on me, O you my friends, for the hand of God has touched me! Why do you, like God, pursue me? Why are you not satisfied with my flesh?" Let God do the pursuing!

In this, too, he finds his echo in many today who have some knowledge of God but who are gripped by the "sickness unto death," in despair because they are estranged from Him.

So all through the drama there is a contradiction in this man which betrays the utter confusion of his mind. He condemns the justice of God; yet he expects God to acquit him. In one of the later chapters he says, "Oh, that I knew where I might find Him, that I might come even to His seat. I would lay my case before Him and fill my mouth with arguments. I would learn what He would answer me and understand what He would say to me. Would He contend with me in the greatness of His power? No, He would give heed to me. There an up-

right man could reason with Him and I
should be acquitted forever by my Judge."
Again, the paradox: he is condemning the
justice and righteousness of God and yet
demanding that God should vindicate him.
Desperately he seeks a God who forever
eludes his pursuit. Yet always he is terrified
by the overwhelming presence of his God.
He demands recognition of his own worth;
he does not ask for mercy. Oh, yes, he asks
for mercy with a view to the alleviation of
his immediate sufferings. Nowhere all
through the record does this man ask for
mercy upon himself as a rebel against God.
That is the root of his sickness unto death.
That is why he is in utter despair. And that
is in large measure characteristic of the
time in which we live.

3

Unsatisfactory Orthodoxy
or
Fallible Fundamentalism

As if to bring Job's sickness-unto-death into sharp relief, its symptoms are displayed in dialogue, debate and rebuttal. For his three friends, after keeping a sensible and sympathetic silence, as some would have it, for seven days—no mean test of friendship—negated the help they might have given and were found, each in his own way, blundering with the truth.

Each friend is a character in his own right. Eliphaz would seem to be the eldest of the group. Characterized always by courtesy, he is the gentleman of them all. There is a certain sensitiveness about Eliphaz. We cannot help admiring the man as we read what he has to say.

Bildad, the second, is argumentative. He wants to fight. He loves a fight. He is cer-

tain that he is right, certain that he will
win, and he is bristling and ready for the
fray.

The last, Zophar, is blunt to the point of
rudeness, laconic beside the others. Each is
a well-defined character.

Job's outbreak of passionate complaint
is their signal for action. There follow in
dramatic sequence three cycles of argument. Eliphaz speaks and Job replies. Bildad speaks and Job replies. Zophar speaks
and Job answers him. A second time the
same sequence occurs, and a third. Only on
the third occasion, Zophar has nothing to
say. The last speaker has become gracious
enough or is baffled enough to keep quiet
and let Job give his final answer.

To summarize these arguments: When
Job has lamented and cursed his day, and
by implication has blamed God for the
whole thing, then Eliphaz, with the utmost
courtesy, enunciates a great dogma: the
dogma that God is just—that He is a righteous God, that He is "too wise to err and
too good to be unkind." Eliphaz admits
that human suffering is a great mystery. He
himself hasn't the key to it, except in indi-

vidual cases. And in the individual case of Job it is very evident, from his rebellious spirit, that Job is suffering because of his own sin. Therefore Eliphaz emphasizes the duty of Job to confess his sin to God, to get right with God, to seek the grace of an offended Deity.

As soon as he pauses, Job bursts into a reply in which it seems as though he is ignoring his friends, ignoring the argument to which he has just listened. He speaks to God and to his own soul of the weight of anguish that he is bearing, of the fact that to him death would be a boon, and of the failure, both of his earthly friends and of God Himself. Now, turning at length to those friends, he first tells them what he thinks of them, and then expresses his utter hopelessness in the face of all that has befallen him. Yet, quite characteristic of human beings, no sooner has he spoken of his complete despair than he cries out in prayer to God, a prayer characterized partly by defiance, partly by bewilderment, but also by desperate pleading for God's mercy upon him.

At that moment, Bildad steps forward,

He is ready for an argument and Job has given him plenty of ground for it. Bildad re-emphasizes the lesson of the Divine justice that Eliphaz has already pointed out. He traces that justice in history as "His story"; that is, the story of God's dealings with men. History records, so he emphasizes, that when men have been good, God has loved them, and His love has been evident in the easy time that they have enjoyed. Bildad himself is having an easy time, and therefore is able to speak without hesitation.

Job replies. He acknowledges the guilt of mankind, but says that God is utterly indifferent to men, whether guilty or innocent, whether man of God or man of the devil. It makes no difference. God is beyond and above humanity, and He neither knows nor, if He knows, does He care.

Zophar, the blunt, speaks then, and says in effect: "Look Job, it's no use dodging the issue. I know that you are skilful in argument. You have been able to reply to Eliphaz. You have been able to put up a worthy battle with Bildad, but come clean, man! You know perfectly well that you are a sinner or these things wouldn't have happened to you. Now confess your sin. You are facing, not a man but the infinite God, and it is time that you recognized it. It is time for you to be converted and to bring forth fruit meet for repentance."

That is his argument. Job's reply to him constitutes a criticism of Providence. It simply is not true, he says, that the really good invariably prosper, while the evil are always punished in this life. So again he defies his friends and he defies God, ending with a great lamentation concerning the fate of man. That is the first cycle of the argument.

As Job pauses for breath, Eliphaz, still in all courtesy, takes the floor to accuse Job of three things. First, that he is guilty of self-incrimination. All that he says in defense of himself is in defiance of God. It is evidence that he is a sinner, that he deserves his punishment. He incriminates, he condemns himself by his very words. Secondly, that Job is characterized by self-delusion. He thinks of himself as wholly innocent and righteous. He is not, he cannot be. Therefore he is deceiving himself.

Eliphaz might have paraphrased the words
of the Apostle Paul and said: "Don't fool
yourself, you can't fool God—whatsoever a
man soweth, that shall he also reap." If you
are reaping corruption, Job, it is very evident that you *are* corrupt, you have been
sowing the seeds of corruption." Thirdly,
according to Eliphaz, Job is guilty of self-
assertion, for he dares to assert his right
against the right of God. Finally and still
courteously, Eliphaz depicts the horrible
fate of the man of evil, "sinful man in the
hands of an angry God."

Job replies briefly: "Miserable comforters are you all." And God is no better; He
is hostile. I am innocent and yet I am in the
abysmal misery that you see.

In his turn, the argumentative Bildad
preaches a "hell-fire-and-damnation" ser-
mon to Job. Job isn't having any, and says
in effect: "If this is so, then your God is
my devil"—to quote the words of John
Wesley. "Your God is characterized by unrighteousness, by enmity. All I am experiencing is from His hostility and the hostility of man." Then suddenly there flames
out that great word: "But, I *know* that my

Redeemer liveth, and He shall stand some
day upon the earth."

Zophar again has his turn and bluntly
speaks of the emptiness of the life of the
godless: "That is what you are experiencing
now, Job, old man! It has caught up with
you and you are discovering how utterly
empty your life has been." But Job, in his
reply, emphasizes his honesty and the cour-
age of that honesty. Yet he also speaks of
the uselessness of prayer. The heavens are
as brass and prayer has no answer. That
completes, in summary, the second cycle of
argument.

The third cycle opens with Eliphaz.
"God does not need either man's work or
His own gifts," is the gist of his argument.
Job must get a sense of proportion. He
seems to think that he is important in the
scheme of things, but God does not need
him. So he proceeds to catalogue Job's
shortcomings. He talks also of the monot-
ony of sin, its dreary fruitlessness. In the
long run, not in so pronounced a manner
always, sin ends as it is ending in the case
of Job. This time, too, Eliphaz calls Job to
repentance and conversion.

Job replies by ignoring his friends and
turning again to God, "Oh that I knew
where I might find *Him*." Then he speaks
of God, as paying no heed to his prayer and
permitting evil to triumph everywhere. Bildad interrupts at this point; but even a man
who loves an argument cannot get very far
if his opponent keeps repeating the same
thing and he himself has nothing new to
offer. Bildad merely says again what he has
said before. And Job merely repeats what
he has said before. As for Zophar, he has
given it up as a bad job; he has no more to
say, and that is the end of the third cycle
of argument.

When the friends have lapsed into silence
from which they should never have
emerged in the first place, Job speaks again.
He discusses true wisdom. When we talk of
the philosophy of the Bible, we should
always remember that it is far different
from any merely earthly philosophy. The
purely human philosopher always begins
with an inquiry, a question mark. He can
assume nothing. Well, if one begins with a
minus quantity, he will end with a minus
quantity. Starting with a question mark, he

ends with an interrogation mark and is still
questioning. Biblical philosophy, on the
contrary, begins with an assertion, in fact,
with two assertions. It starts with two
premises and from them draws conclusions.
The worldly philosopher says, "That is the
very thing we cannot do. We can assume
nothing." But that is precisely why he never gets anywhere.

But the Bible philosopher begins with
this: "God is!" There is a God. And by
definition, if there is a God, then all wisdom resides in Him. Ergo, "the fear of the
Lord is the beginning of wisdom." If you
want to be wise, you will rightly relate
yourself to God. Again, wisdom in the Old
Testament does not range the realm of the
hypothetical; it always means knowing how
to live aright, practical skill in the ordering
of one's life and the developing of one's
character. That is wisdom according to the
Bible. And Job, now speaking to God and
turning away from his friends, asks the
question: Where may such wisdom be
found? In words that might have been written yesterday he asks of science—the science of his day, true, but the principle still

applies—if wisdom is really to be found
there. Knowledge is a-plenty. But Job turns
from it, and he says: No, I find there is no
wisdom there. He turns to religion, to theology, to religious technique, and he says
that it is all equally futile. Only as he looks
to God is he able to say that He alone
understands the way to wisdom, and that
man, in turning to God, will find wisdom in
Him and Him alone.

Yet, even now, Job does not turn whole-
heartedly to God. Instead, in self-pity, he
indulges himself in memories of happier
times. He reviews, too, the misery of the
present, and, by contrast, the misery becomes deeper and more poignant. He con-
cludes with a final declaration of his own
innocence. That part of the drama is ended.
The friends are heard no more and Job
himself is silent.

But someone else steps forward. All the
time, a young man has been there. In those
days young men kept quiet, but young men
in those days had no more happiness in
keeping quiet than they have today. This
young man, Elihu, had stood or sat there
listening to Eliphaz with his courteous

phrases, his poetic philosophy, his marvel-
lously soothing approach to Job's problems
while he does not understand them in the
least. Apparently Elihu has fretted and
fumed within himself, saying, "The silly
old fool." And when Job replies to Eliphaz
and then to Bildad and again to Zophar,
the young man says, "He's got it all wrong.
I wish I could say my piece. I'd set him
right. And Bildad and Zophar are no better
than Eliphaz; they are silly old fools too."
But they have now been put to rout, they
have been silenced finally. Job has had his
last say and now the young man is able to
step forward and utter the contemporary
voice. Today we would call him The Angry
Young Man. That is what he was, completely disgusted with the older generation. But
when he has had his say and completed his
argument, he has not added one solitary
thing to what the three older men have
said. In fact, I was almost going to say, he
does not say a solitary thing, period! Elihu
has nothing new to say. His statements are
beautifully worded, but when you finish
reading I doubt very much if you can tell
me *what* he said. He is only repeating the

others' arguments in "modern" terms. Certainly he is repeating them in the language that his own generation understands! But there is nothing new about it. And that is why *God* suddenly speaks.

Perhaps the most puzzling aspect of this book to the Christian who reads it dutifully in the course of his devotions is its condemnation of men who say so many good and true things. Each of them exalts the greatness, wisdom, power, and justice of God. Each is scandalized by Job's cries of futility and despair, by his persistent assertions of personal righteousness. Each is impeccably orthodox. How could men so right be so utterly wrong? Yet that they were is certainly the verdict of this book. In our examination of their psychology and reasoning, we may possibly discover an answer to much that puzzles us in the endless debating of today, perhaps much to convict us in our smug assumptions and judgments.

In order to exalt the Divine glory, they emphasize the great divide, the impassable gulf, between God and man—even between God and His angels. "Can mortal man be righteous before God? Can a man be pure

before his Maker? Even in His servants He
puts no trust, and His angels He charges
with error. . . . the heavens are not clean
in His sight. How much less one who is
abominable and corrupt, a man who drinks
iniquity like water." "Behold even the
moon is not bright and the stars are not
clean in His sight. How much less man, who
is a maggot, and the son of man, who is a
worm." So Eliphaz and Bildad, though very
different in personality, agree in doctrine.
And they are right!

Yet they are wrong, for in their busy
safeguarding of the absolute freedom of
God they make unwarranted statements.
Waiving the irony of the generality that
"even in His servants He puts no trust"—in
view of the particularity of God's question
to Satan: "Hast thou considered my servant Job?"—Eliphaz surely passes the
bounds of human presumption by asking:
"Is it any pleasure to the Almighty if you
are righteous, or is it gain to Him if you
make your ways blameless? Is it for your
fear of Him that He reproves you and en-
ters into judgment with you?"

Again they are quite right in insisting

that Job's sin lies in his proud refusal to
acknowledge the limitations of his creature-
liness. "Are you the first man that was
born? Or were you brought forth before
the hills? Have you listened in the Council
of God? And do you limit wisdom to yourself?" But how arrogantly wrong they were
in considering his misfortune as nemesis, as
the inevitable, pursuing result of sins, his
children's and his own: "If your children
have sinned against Him, He has delivered
them into the power of their transgressions.
If iniquity is in your hand put it far away,
and let not wickedness dwell in your
tents." And after a too graphic description
of Job's condition—"Surely such are the
dwellings of the ungodly, such the place of
him who knows not God." Again, yet more
bluntly: "Is not your wickedness great?
There is no end to your iniquities. For you
have exacted pledges of your brothers for
nothing and stripped the naked of their
clothing. You have given no water to the
weary to drink and have withheld bread
from the hungry." Baseless assumptions all
of them, refuted by Job in chapter twenty-
nine, and—though they could not know

it—by God Himself in His description of His servant.

Again they are right in urging Job to seek God with humility and trust: "As for me, I would seek God, and to God would I commit my cause." "If you will seek God and make supplication to the Almighty." "If you set your heart aright you will stretch out your hands before Him." "Agree with God and be at peace; thereby good will come to you."

But they are completely wrong in their philosophy of mechanical retribution, of poetic justice, of impersonal law always verified in historical experience. "The wicked man writhes in pain all his days . . . he is destined for the sword . . . he wanders abroad for bread, saying, 'Where is it?' Yea the light of the wicked is put out. . . . This is the portion of a wicked man with God . . . if his children are multiplied it is for the sword, and his offspring have not enough to eat. He goes to bed rich, but will do so no more; he opens his eyes and his wealth is gone."

Their heresy in these easy generalizations is Job's own fundamental mistake—

moralism: the virtue-is-always-rewarded-
vice-always-punished concept of God's
dealings. But Job is alone with his error in
the midst of the demonstration of its failure. They are but onlookers and their pat
judgments, by whatever right motives
prompted, show the vast lacunae in their
knowledge.

There is no room in their theology, be it
observed, for Divine grace, for the unmer-
ited outflowing of God's love toward the
unworthy and helpless. Nor does their concept of virtue leave any room for man's
pure love of God—for the love that lingers
and wrestles when all understanding is gone
and communion rudely shattered. Rather,
religion for them is a bargain in which
humility is the best policy and morality the
purchase price of peace of mind.

They have, it is true, a magnificent
creed, orthodox and lofty. Not only theists,
they are also monotheists, and their one
God is great, wise, powerful and just. Nev-
ertheless their belief is not true faith. They
walk by sight and insist that seeing is believing; they refuse, in fact, to consider
explanations not based on the theory of

swift and inevitable return for virtue or vice. Their orthodoxy rapidly becomes— have we not seen it and shared in it?—a source of personal pride. "Surely *we* are the people"—thus they might have argued with Job's scornful accusation. It is not God in fact whom they are defending, but their own security. For if Job *is* righteous and yet so stricken, of what value or security then is *their* uprightness?

The repeated strictures on judging, found in the Gospels and Epistles of the New Testament, may well have the type of Job's "comforters" in mind. Without the genuine humility of "looking to thyself lest thou also be tempted" they arrogate to themselves the office of the Vicar of God, able to speak ex cathedra to the sinner.

There is little or no evidence of the milk of human kindness in their attitude—a fact that wrings from Job such words as: "He who withholds kindness from a friend forsakes the fear of the Almighty." "In the thought of one who is at ease there is contempt for misfortune."

These "friends" are the "secure," the ones who, instead of being in the hand of

God, "bring their God in their hand," that
is, they appear to regard Him as their possession by desert and inalienable right.

Such theological sin on the part of the
orthodox, the fundamentalists, has a para-
doxical function in this strange, perennially
fresh and trenchant story. It sharpens the
quest of the condemned "heretic," driving
him into a frantic search for light. Refusing
to be documented, rejecting their pat cata-
loguing, conscious in all his rebellion and
despair that the last word is not with them,
Job turns and turns and turns again to the
God who hides Himself. "Lo my eye has
seen all this, my ear has heard and under-
stood it," he says in the orthodox, theological statement with which he has matched
theirs, "What you know, I also know; I am
not inferior to you. But I would speak to
the Almighty and I desire to argue my case
with God."

By this very attitude, by the concentrated, naked desperation of his search, he is
transformed into a herald of truths hitherto
concealed or unknown. It is one of the
shattering paradoxes of human experience
that even the injustice of those whom we

had accounted friends and who considered that they were expressing their "friendship" in the perpetration of that very injustice, is used by the Judge of all the earth to our betterment—if only we will permit it to be so. In Job's case, their misunderstanding, their self-righteous and sadistic strictures, their censorious sermonizing, accentuating the torture of a righteous man's soul, were able so to vitalize his spiritual dynamic, so to intensify the penetrative depth of his vision of the eternal realities, that the victim, who had resembled nothing so much as the hero of a Greek tragedy, was transformed into a prophet inspired by the Eternal Spirit.

4

The Necessity of a Mediator

The three friends of Job, and the fourth, the young man, representative of the contemporary generation, all had been given their irrefutable replies. They were completely orthodox, they were fundamentalists in their theology, they knew all the answers—yet they were as wrong as men could possibly be. Such men often are when they are faced with a real human problem. In other words, when a man of God, a man of moral rectitude, of high principles and of integrity as Job was, undergoes such agony as he experienced, human thought lacks knowledge of the underlying causes. It can but confuse things; it can only "darken counsel." There is one solution alone. That lies in the intimate,

first-hand experience of the sufferer with
God Himself.

Sometimes in their utter and disconso-
late solitude among their fellows, men driv-
en into abysmal depths discover there a
comforting solitude with God. I once knew
a man who had been an incorrigible sinner,
who in his late middle life, while serving a
term in Sing Sing prison, found Christ
through the Gideon Bible in his cell. In
utter destitution, in moral bankruptcy and
spiritual poverty, with no friends even in
his own family, in solitary confinement,
serving the last month of a long sentence,
he found his refuge in God. His lonely cell
was illumined by the very radiance of heav-
en; but that was not so with Job. Job's
loneliness was the more acute as he became
the more conscious of standing before God.
He never was so much alone as when he
was referring to the Almighty. Friends had
failed him, his own wife found him abhor-
rent, his family and all his acquaintances
were gone, and at that very time the God
he needed became a stranger to him.

There are very many whose hearts re-

echo "To me, God is dead. In my experience He isn't real. He does not manifest
Himself. He is a stranger and I am estranged
from Him. The heavens are as brass—my
prayers get nowhere. God is dead!" That
attitude is characteristic of Job throughout
his complaint. Time and time again it is the
confession that perforce he makes. Yet a
luminous thread runs all the way through
the book, and all the way through Job's
confessions, through his innermost feelings
and reactions.

In the old days of the British Navy, they
say, every rope had a thread of scarlet
running through it. It was the Navy's way
of keeping track of its possessions. Anyone
who saw a length of rope containing a
thread of scarlet knew that the rope had
been stolen from the British Navy. Similarly, running all through the Book of Job,
despite the pessimism, despite the despondency of utter despair, nonetheless this
thread of light recurs whenever the Spirit
moves Job to utter some great words of
praise or of faith—however soon doomed to
fall silent.

Slowly, almost imperceptibly, Job's self-sufficiency was broken down. He recognized in his confession that he could not bridge the gulf between God and Himself. Job had been self-righteous, justifiably so in the face of human judgment because he *was* righteous; but he dared to be arrogant even before God. That arrogance had not entirely departed, but slowly, surely, self-sufficiency was collapsing. He realized the abyss stretching between God and himself. Seemingly, there was no connection, no fellowship between them, and Job began to realize that if the gulf was to be bridged it must be from God's side and not from his. That was a tremendous advance. He was still in the slough of despond; he was still steeped in his own despair—a pessimist of pessimists. God failed to furnish practical help to him. Job had no comfort from His presence. There was an unbridgeable gulf. Thank God it is unbridgeable! Job had thought that he could bridge it; at last he realized that, if it was to be bridged, God alone could do it.

The paradox of faith prevented his believing that God would finally abandon him. Here, recognizably true to human nature, is a tremendous experience in the emotions of Job and in his insight.

I cite certain features of it: first the strange irony of a hope that is thwarted as soon as entertained. For instance: "Why dost Thou not pardon my transgressions and take away my iniquities? From now on I shall lie in the earth. Thou wilt seek me but I shall not be."

That is, I think, one of the most startling, the most daring things that even Job says! It is the idea that God Himself is groping in the darkness for a creature who is lost, but that He is doing so too late. Somehow there is confidence that God is able to forgive, able to cleanse, able to restore, because He is God. He will, therefore, at last stretch forth His hand toward this man—BUT it will be too late! Job expects, threatens almost, that he will be dead before the Divine help arrives.

These Old Testament characters were commonly far more honest than you and I are. How they dared to talk out in the presence of God their doubts and fears, their skepticism, their unbelief, their sense of being themselves just, and consequently of God's injustice! When men are honest in the presence of God, there is hope for them. True, these words were an expression of Job's self-pity; yet underlying them was the conviction that there is a God who cares, even though He does not care enough to put Himself out in order to help His creatures or, alternatively, that He is powerless to do so.

Another feature is Job's remarkable awareness of man's impotence regarding his own salvation. "If I wash myself with snow and cleanse my hands with lye, yet Thou wilt plunge me into the pit and mine own will abhor me." Which is to say, "I may do everything I can to cleanse myself, yet I shall still remain filthy and can expect judgment."

Once more, against the absolute will of God, every human attempt at clearance miscarries, simply because God is God! The writer of Ecclesiastes says, "God is in Heaven, thou upon earth; therefore let thy words be few." We are unable to span that impassable gulf, to bridge it, to attain His presence. God remains God, and we remain of the earth, earthy. Even Job cried: "He is

not a man as I am that I might answer Him;
He is not a man as I am that we should
come to trial together." I have a great complaint, for a fearful thing has befallen me,
an agonizing, continuing and ever worsen-
ing experience; yet my Adversary is One
infinitely removed from me. By His very
nature I am unable to come near Him. If
He were a man against whom I had a claim,
we could enter court together, we could
call upon a human judge to decide between
us. But here there is no one who has any-
thing in common with the two of us, who
is able to put one hand on God, the other
on me—there is no umpire. The old English
word in the King James Version is a very
unusual one, "There is no Daysman between us." The word literally means, one
who reasons, who reproves, who decides.
That is what I need, Job says, between God
and myself: one who will reason with God
and me. To the Prophet Isaiah, the Spirit of
God says: "Come now, let us reason together, saith the Lord." Job knew nothing of
this but he did know that he needed one to
stand between God and himself, to reason
with God and to reason with him, and in

reasoning, bring them both together; one who could reprove Job, put his life to the test, demonstrate where he was wrong. Yes, and Job even thought of the possibility of his demonstrating where God was wrong! He, the Daysman, would be able finally to decide this wrong. Oh, that there were a Daysman, one who might lay his hand upon us both, bringing us together, and reconciling us!

We can pause to be reminded that where the Old Testament cry is "Oh, that I knew where I might find Him," the New Testament answers: "Thou hast found Him, He has been revealed." "Oh, that there were an umpire, a daysman, a mediator, between God and me." "There *is* a Mediator between God and man, Himself man, Christ Jesus."

A solemnly strange note sounds in the book from time to time, because Job is sure that he is on the verge of death. Certainly no one would have offered much for his life. A disease was evidently eating away his body. It may have been, as some have suggested, black leprosy. At any rate, it was something horrible, something destructive,

almost obscene, and he often speaks as
though he were a dying man.

So, it is suggested, "If there is no daysman, no mediator in this life, can there be a
sequel? Can there be an afterlife?" Do we
realize the significance? Job had said, in the
seventh chapter, "I shall lie in the earth;
Thou wilt seek me but I shall not be." Yet
again he cried, "O that Thou wouldst hide
me in Sheol"—the place of the departed—
"that Thou wouldst conceal me until Thy
wrath departs, that Thou wouldst appoint
me a set time and remember me."

I wonder if we feel the force of those
sentences. Such references are very rare in
the Old Testament. Admittedly, the psalmist says, "I have kept the Lord always before me; because He is at my right hand I
shall not be moved. Therefore my heart is
glad and my soul rejoices. My body dwells
secure. For Thou dost not give me up to
Hell nor suffer Thy godly one to see de-
struction. Thou dost show me the path of
life; in Thy presence is fullness of joy, and
at Thy right hand are pleasures forever-
more." And again, "I am continually with
Thee; Thou dost hold my right hand, Thou

dost guide me with Thy counsel and after-
wards Thou wilt receive me to glory. Whom
have I in Heaven but Thee, and there is
none upon earth that I desire beside Thee.
My flesh and my heart may fail, but God is
the strength of my heart and my portion
forever." But these are rare and exception-
al, for, generally speaking, all through the
Old Testament, with regard to the future
there is the gloom of non-revelation. Very
occasionally there are flashes of insight
such as the ones that I have quoted. The
marvel of it is that out of the depths such
flashes are given to Job.

And yet the hope faded almost as soon
as it was expressed. Another of the great
psalms asks, "Dost Thou work wonders for
the dead? Do the shades rise up to praise
Thee? Is Thy steadfast love declared in the
grave or Thy faithfulness in the place of the
departed? Are Thy wonders known in the
darkness or Thy saving health in the land of
forgetfulness?" A negative reply is antici-
pated, and such is the Old Testament out-
look in the face of death.

That reaction occurred with Job. "It is
too good to be true," he said. "There must

be a sequel—but no, there can't be. There must be something after death, something beyond my apprehension, something I am not to see in this life. And yet, actually there is no hope." It is characteristic of the man, characteristic of *man*, this swinging from one extreme to the other. So, thank God, the theme of the daysman, the mediator, recurs. Beyond all the miseries of the present, he saw the face of the heavenly witness. Just after he had cried, "O earth, cover not my blood and let my cry find no resting place"—in other words, this evil thing, this thing without justification that is happening to me, let not this just be blotted out and forgotten; there must be vindication for the man of God—he immediately went on to say, "Even now, see, my Witness is in heaven and He that voucheth for me is on high. My friends scorn me, my eye pours out tears to God that He would maintain the right of a man with God and that of a man with his neighbor." My Witness is on high. What did he mean? Did he KNOW what he meant? I doubt it. It was a cry wrought out, *not* in his intelligence, but in the depths of his being; it was the cry of his entire emotional nature. It must be, he was sure, if there is not witness to my righteousness here on earth, that there is One in Heaven who will bear witness to me.

Once again we are reminded of that tremendous word about One who is touched with the feeling of our infirmities, One who was put to the test in all points even as we are, our merciful and faithful High Priest, the One who ever lives to make intercession for us.

He ever lives above, for me to intercede.
His all-redeeming love, His precious blood to plead.
His blood atoned for all our race,
And sprinkles now the Throne of Grace.

"O earth, cover not my blood and let my cry find no resting place." "See, my Witness is in heaven and He that voucheth for me is on high." There came a greater, more exultant cry: "I know that my Redeemer lives, and at last He will stand for me upon the earth. And after this skin of mine has been destroyed, without this flesh shall I see God. I shall see Him on my side, and mine eyes shall behold Him, and not as a stranger."

"My Redeemer liveth!" His fellows have all failed him, as he said. Not only had his fellows failed him, but vindication in a future generation was no particular comfort to him. I can never understand those who say, "I believe in immortality, in the sense that we live again in our children and in the generations to come." Much comfort that is to me! I may be a very selfish person. I may have very little of the father instinct, but I have little interest in living again in my children, whatever that means! I want experience of my own that I myself can savor and enjoy. That is what Job implies here when he cries, "I know that my Redeemer lives!"

The word "Redeemer," the Hebrew word *goel,* literally means kinsman-redeemer. If a man were sold into slavery in ancient Israel, thereby forfeiting his house and property, it was the responsibility of his nearest of kin to purchase back both the slave and the property, to re-establish the man in his own inheritance. It is the

word used in the story of Ruth where Bo-
az, anxious to marry his young kinswoman-
by-marriage, remembers that there is a
nearer kinsman who has the first right to be
the *goel*. Using this same word Job said: "I
know that my *Goel* lives, and at last He
shall stand upon the earth." Did he grasp
the whole significance of what he said?
Surely not, any more than prophets knew
the full significance of their prophecies. He
was simply compelled to burst out with his
heart-cry: "I know that I have a Kinsman-
Redeemer. I don't know how, nor when,
nor the way in which this thing is to be
brought about. My earthly kinsmen have
failed me. No one is able or willing to help.
Yet I believe in God, and I believe that
there is one who will exercise the right for
me, as *Goel.*" And the word is the very
word that describes the Lord Jesus Christ.

Job had no sooner given vent to that cry
of faith than gloom again descended upon
him. How human it all is! How like the
Apostle Andrew coming into the presence
of the Lord Jesus, when a great crowd of
five thousand men, besides women and
children, was present, and all of them hun-

gry. Andrew said, "Lord, there is a little lad
here; he has five loaves and two fishes—but
what is that among so many?" Just for the
moment he had faith to say, "This is what
we have, Lord." But immediately doubt
assailed, "What is that among so many?"

I once heard John McNeill preach on the
episode in which the Lord walked on the
water, and Peter went out of the boat
across the water to meet Him. Then, beginning to sink, he cried, "Lord save me."
John McNeill said: "This world's wisdom
says 'Second thoughts are best.' It is not
true in eternal matters; first thoughts are
best. Peter's first thought was to walk to
the Lord. His second thought was to
drown."

Job's first thought was that he had a
Redeemer who would vindicate him, that
he had a witness in heaven. All of earth had
failed him, he was helpless in himself, but
God would surely redeem him. But "listen
carefully to my word," he went on to say,
"and let this be your consolation"—in
speaking to these ultra-fundamentalist
friends of his, these self-righteous friends
who knew all the answers—"Bear with me

and I will speak, and after I have spoken, mock on. As for me, is my complaint against man? Why should I not be impatient?"—and so he returns to his ranting against the injustice of God.

"O that I knew where I might find Him, that I might come even to His seat. I would set my cause in order before Him and fill my mouth with argument; I'd learn what He would answer me and understand what He would say to me. Would He contend with me in the greatness of His power? No, there the upright man might reason with Him and I should be acquitted forever by my Judge." There is much of the old self-righteousness left there, but it is passing.

"From out of the populous city men groan, and the soul of the wounded crieth out. Yet God regardeth not the folly." This is exactly where you and I have often come. We have believed; in the depths we have cried unto God, and out of the depths God has revealed Himself to us; but the light has been eclipsed and gloom has once again descended. We tell ourselves that we must be realistic after all. What hope is there? What possibility is there? In the next life, perhaps, but in this life almost certainly none. God does not hear us.

Yet the luminous thread runs through the book, until at last God vindicates Himself in and to His servant Job. He brings him to the place of solitude and silence. The storm of adversity is over; the storm of criticism and opposition has subsided; the storms of youth's scorn and age's sententiousness have both been quelled by God. The self-righteous humbug—paradoxically also a great man of integrity—is fed up with himself. At long last he is willing to let God speak to him. Now, when Job loses all desire to vindicate himself, he discovers his rest and his peace, his joy and his prosperity, his ability to bring joy and blessing into other lives. He has never found that before. He loses all sense of his own righteousness, all sense of his deserving better at the Lord's hand than this. He loses it at that very moment when he cries: "I have heard of Thee by the hearing of the ear, now mine eye seeth Thee; wherefore I abhor myself and repent in dust and ashes."

5

The Sufficiency of Grace

Before God's ultimate dealings with him, Job's last word to God was the final answer of the natural, even of the religious man. "Let the Almighty answer me." One would say that Job had adequate reason to make such demand of God. All through the succeeding centuries, his sufferings and deprivations, the extreme pressure of events upon him, have made him an example of undeserved suffering. Mankind would respond with Job, "Let the Almighty answer me." That is, "What is the explanation of this? I have a right to demand a reason from God!"

Now, the Divine answer is always quite different from the human expectation. God through the Prophet Isaiah says, "My thoughts are not your thoughts, neither are your ways My ways; for as the heavens are higher than the earth, so are My ways higher than your ways and My thoughts than your thoughts." It is the great desire of the Apostle Paul that in all things God should be vindicated. "Yea, let God be true but every man a liar." God DOES answer, but He never answers in accordance with our expectation. God's method with man is revealed by our Lord Jesus Christ. We find in the Gospels that, almost without exception when men questioned Jesus of Nazareth, He either did not reply at all, or His reply seemed to have no connection with their question! Or again, He answered them with another question. Almost invariably he refused to answer them as they expected. In that, during the days of His flesh, He was demonstrating the method of His Heavenly Father. God never answers the demand of man. For God's answer consists not in giving replies but in asking questions.

"Then the Lord answered Job out of the whirlwind, 'Who is this that darkeneth counsel by words without knowledge? You, Job, gird up your loins like a man!' " In other words, "Don't be a baby, whining in self-pity. I will question you and you shall answer me." That is God's answer to Job's demand: Be a man and not a baby. Be a man and not a moron. Don't expect me to answer your questions. *I* am going to question you, and in the inquisition you will learn the answers and reply to My questions—I am God. God does not for man's satisfaction, even though that man be writhing in agony, explain the mysteries of the universe.

Pascal, one of the greatest minds of the centuries, spoke of man's "misery and grandeur"; that man is the tool of circumstance, that he is infinitesimally small, that he suffers and is characterized by misery. Yet also, to quote another philosopher, "Know thy dread nature, a creature yet a cause," sharing something of the grandeur of the Creator Himself. God does not stoop to explain all the mysteries of the universe to his inquiring saints. Nor does He solve, philosophically, the problems of pain and agony, frustration, deprivation and evil. Many of the old commentators said that the theme of the Book of Job is "Why do the godly suffer?" If it is, then in characteristic manner God does not answer the question. And from one end of the Bible to the other, you will find no answer to it. God does not pander to our curiosity. He does not solve for us *in time* the problem of evil.

Neither does God publicly vindicate His servant. Job may live all his life, even though his fortunes are restored, without any demonstration that in all outward matters he had been righteous. God says so in the record itself; but many or most of his fellows may go on misjudging Job to the end of their days.

Men object to this lack of vindication in cynicism, in what they call atheism. Skeptically they say: "Surely God, if there be a God, does not act in this way. Surely, the dignity of human nature demands more of God than this. Or, if this *is* the experience of a man who gives himself to righteousness, then there is no percentage in it!" So men echo the cynicism of Satan himself.

Or they profess atheism in the face of such facts. I have often said—and I have never seen any reason to retract the statement—that I do not believe there is such a creature as an atheist on the face of the earth. I do not believe there ever has been an atheist, or that there ever will be one— that is to say, a man who does not basically, initially, believe in the existence of *a* God. Yes, practical atheists there are by the millions, men who live lives in which they ignore God. "The fool hath said in his heart, No God." That is, I'll have nothing to do with God. Even the fool does not say, as our English version has it, "There is no God." But in these matters men respond to what they feel is the injustice of the situation. The tragic sense of life calls for such response. It was not so with Job.

Notice—and in noting remember the skeptics' mockery of it—the anthropomorphism of the passages in which God is represented as replying to Job. To be anthropomorphic, the skeptic would explain, is to represent God as though He were a man and to talk, in ignorance and folly, about the arm of the Lord and the eyes of the Lord and so on. But how else can we talk about God so that human beings may understand Him? There is no other way. So ultimately, when God would express Himself in perfection, He himself became Man.

Only in that way could we understand
Him.

Yes, God is represented as uttering human words to respond to Job. His commu-
nication renders Job aware of the greatness,
the transcendence of God, the fact that he
is dealing with the Creator and Sustainer of
the universe. God reveals Himself as the
One who "makes grass to grow in the
places where no man is," who creates the
useless things, the utterly extravagant
things, who is the Source of the extrava-
gance of nature. It seems as though God is
saying that this very spendthriftiness of His
is the demonstration of His freedom, the
demonstration that He *is* God and that His
resources can never be plumbed, never be
measured. Job is being overwhelmed by the
sheer greatness and infinitude of God.

It isn't fair, we say. Perhaps man has
such an exalted opinion of his own impor-
tance in these days, of his own value, that
in this way alone can he be brought to
terms with God and with his own soul. For
at the same time, God makes Job aware of
His immanence. He steps toward the creature of His hands. He grants him a vision of

the Divine glory, and "Job is raised from the prison into the windswept pageant of the universe. He leaves the enclosure of his aching self and discovers a world." That is what he needs. It is said of the prodigal son that "he came to himself." Job had not come to himself yet. He was living in a concentrated world, strictly limited. He was, as a matter of fact, not all there. Neither is any one of us by nature, especially when we sit in judgment upon God.

G. K. Chesterton speaks with remarkable perspicacity—and, for that matter, perspicuity—about the maniac. I earnestly believe that the unregenerate mind is that of a madman. This madness is characteristic of Job in the passages we have been considering. Chesterton says: "The madman is not a man who has lost his reason. The madman is the man who has lost everything except his reason."

> The madman's explanation of a thing is always complete, and often in a purely rational sense, satisfactory. His mind moves in a perfect but narrow circle. A small circle is quite as infinite as a large circle; but although it is quite as infinite, it is not so

large. In the same way the insane explanation is quite as complete as the sane one, but
it is not so large. A bullet is quite as round as
the world, but it is not the world. There is
such a thing as a narrow universality; there is
such a thing as a small and cramped eternity;
you may see it in many modern religions.
Now, speaking quite externally and empir-
ically, we may say that the strongest and
most unmistakable *mark* of madness is this
combination between a logical completeness
and a spiritual contraction. If you and I were
dealing with a mind that was growing mor-
bid, we should be chiefly concerned not so
much to give it arguments as to give it air, to
convince that there was something cleaner
and cooler outside the suffocation of a single
argument.

That, I think, was precisely Job's situation, and it is exactly the situation of the
modern man, often of the modern Christian. Job is brought face to face with a God
who is infinite and eternal and all-powerful,
yet a God who is intimately interested in
him, the creature. Consequently—I love to
repeat it—"he is raised from the prison into
the windswept pageant of the universe; he
leaves the enclosure of his aching self and
he discovers a world."

Now, will this man condemn God in
order that he himself may be justified? For
the second time God speaks. "Then God
answered Job out of the whirlwind, 'Gird
up your loins like a man. I will question
you and you will declare to Me.' " He has
said that already: "Job, quit living only for
yourself, sensing only your own needs and
demanding the fulfilment of them." God
has revealed something of His magnifi-
cence, but also, in revealing it, His intimate
interest in the man to whom He reveals it;
and having done so, once again He says,
"Gird up your loins like a man. I will
question you and you shall answer me. Will
you even put Me in the wrong? Will you
condemn Me that you may be justified?"
All through the Scriptures of Truth, and all
through the history of those who have
known the joy of the Lord as their
strength, this experience has been repeated.
When I come to the place where I no longer
demand that God make His ways known to
me, that He satisfy *my* sense of justice and
answer *my* questions, when I am willing to
be questioned by God and reduced by Him
to my proper size, then redemption begins,

then there is real traffic between God and my own soul.

Job learned the lesson of awe, and with that, of wonder.

Rudolf Otto, in his book *The Idea of the Holy,* speaks of the "numinous" and uses as one of his examples the case of Jacob at Bethel. After Jacob had dreamed his dream and God had revealed Himself, then in trembling the patriarch cried, "This is a dreadful place; this is none other than the House of God; this is the gate of Heaven; God is in this place and I did not know it." He had been brought to recognize the presence of God. There are three things to be remarked about that experience: the first is the sense of awe in the presence of the absolute holiness of a righteous God; secondly, the sense of human humility, of correct perspective, of being reduced to scale, of being placed where one belongs in contrast with the holy God; thirdly, the fact that traffic between this God of holiness and the man now humbled in His presence can take place.

That experience, in far greater depth, is

set forth in the Book of Job, and it sweeps on to its conclusion: the sense of awe in the heart of this man. He had never had it before. Oh, he believed in God. He would have told you, with any fundamentalist, that God is infinite and eternal, all-powerful, righteous and just; but Job himself had never been filled with awe in the very presence of God.

Now he is. And with that awe comes a sense of wonder which he knows will never end. Wonder will succeed wonder, as Job comes to know God better: a God who stands above and beyond human traditions, human ideals and human wisdom; a God who is altogether Other, yet a God who bridges the gulf between Himself and man and makes Himself known to man.

Only ignorant presumption will demand that God's justice work according to our puny standards. And Job learns that. He has boasted, "I will come forth like gold that is refined." In other words, all this is going to purify me. So it did, but not in such a manner that Job could boast about it! Now, he who had expected confidently to come forth as gold, bows in adoration and repentance before the God who has revealed Himself to him.

Then Job answered the Lord (what a different answer it is from any that had preceded it): "I know that Thou canst do all things, and that no purpose of Thine can be thwarted. Who is this (you are asking, Lord) that hides counsel without knowledge?" God had asked that first of Elihu but He had also asked it of Job himself.

> Therefore (I acknowledge it is I) I have uttered what I did not understand, things too wonderful for me, which I do not know.
>
> Now hear me (but my speech will be different from what it has ever been before).
>
> I will question You, and You declare unto me.
>
> I had heard of Thee by the hearing of the ear, but now my eye sees Thee;
>
> Therefore I despise myself, and repent in dust and ashes.

And in the presence of this holy God, pain is stilled, grace is revealed as all-sufficient; Job becomes aware of his own sinfulness and his own nothingness; and at that very moment, reconciliation between God and himself is effected. One has said that he is saved at the very moment of surrender. He receives all when he surrenders all. God's judgment opens up to Job His mercy, and the shattered giant no longer attempts to "grasp this sorry scheme of things entire." Now he understands the will of his Sovereign, and the will of his Sovereign is to take him and make him a witness to the holiness and care of the faithful Creator.

When Campbell Morgan produced his commentary on the Book of Hosea, he called it the Heart and Holiness of God. Sometimes we confuse these things. The holiness of God—His righteousness, His justice and His judgment exercised in my life— is something to make me tremble. But it is the heart as well as the holiness of God that is emphasized, and this is what Job himself discovered through his experience.

I have omitted from this consideration the glimpse behind the scenes that is given by revelation. I have omitted it purposely because it was not granted to Job—certainly not until his travail was accomplished.

But surely it was written and has been preserved for our sakes that "through patience and the comfort of the Scriptures we might have hope."

Nowhere in Scripture is a greater honor paid to merely mortal man than this: that he is used to refute the slander of the prototypal Slanderer; that he is used as God's own witness; that God counted on him, through agony and darkness, yet to cling to his Creator.